THE AFFIRMATIONS

THE AFFIRMATIONS

LUKE HATHAWAY

BIBLIOASIS
WINDSOR, ONTARIO

FIRST EDITION

Library and Archives Canada Cataloguing in Publication

Title: The affirmations : poems / Luke Hathaway.
Names: Hathaway, Luke, author.
Identifiers: Canadiana (print) 20210354658 | Canadiana (ebook) 20210354666
    ISBN 9781771964852 (softcover) | ISBN 9781771964869 (ebook)
Subjects: LCGFT: Poetry.
Classification: LCC PS8615.A781975 A69 2022 | DDC C811/.6—dc23

Edited by Jeffery Donaldson
Copy-edited by John Sweet
Text and cover designed by Ingrid Paulson
Cover image by Jon Claytor

Published with the generous assistance of the Canada Council for the Arts, which last year invested $153 million to bring the arts to Canadians throughout the country, and the financial support of the Government of Canada. Biblioasis also acknowledges the support of the Ontario Arts Council (OAC), an agency of the Government of Ontario, which last year funded 1,709 individual artists and 1,078 organizations in 204 communities across Ontario, for a total of $52.1 million, and the contribution of the Government of Ontario through the Ontario Book Publishing Tax Credit and Ontario Creates.

PRINTED AND BOUND IN CANADA

for Daniel Cabena

CONTENTS

A NATIVITY

Past contorted orchard apples,
quickly now, toward where the road
bends sharply to the north, the light
increasing as I go so that
I can't be sure which one of us
illuminates the fence, the horse,
the field held in the crook of hills,
the group of houses—this one? *That one*

where I would arrive, arriving:
what you've carried, leave it here;
what gestures you've prepared, now make them;
whether or not they will suffice,
this is the place where you will turn
toward where, behind *the little mountain*
that humps up in the east, the sky
prepares to loose, at last, by light,

                            the light

In 1940, as war in Europe deepened, the English poet
W.H. Auden—then living in America—wrote a letter, in verse,
to a friend. The result, a long poem with extensive, chatty
annotation, was published in Auden's *New Year Letter* (the
American title was *The Double Man)* in 1941:

> Under the familiar weight
> Of winter, conscience and the State,
> In loose formations of good cheer,
> Love, language, loneliness and fear,
> Towards the habits of next year,
> Along the streets the people flow....

In January 2018, I decided to try my hand at my own verse
letter to a friend, a devotee of Auden, with whom I had been
in conversation in person and in letter around some
of Auden's themes. Auden appears in my letter; so does the
poet Richard Outram, who had died of hypothermia—his
choice—a dozen Januaries earlier, and whose work I was
studying at the time I wrote these lines. There are other
spirits, familiar and unfamiliar—the poet Rilke, the lay-
theologian Charles Williams, one of Bach's unknown
librettists, the great poet Anon...—but for the most part
they are like the guests at a dinner party: one doesn't need to
know their names (I hope) in order to enjoy the conversation.

By the time I finished my *New Year Letter*, Epiphanytide was behind me, and I was well progressed into Ordinary Time; I sent my letter to my friend on 14 February, writing:

I think it's Valéry who said works of art aren't ever finished, only at last abandoned. It turns out verse letters aren't ever finished, only at last sent. Here's mine, for you. I send it on the Saint's day, the old god having been otherwise banished from the liturgical calendar. But the occasion, as you will see, is Auden's. With love.

1 – 25 January 2018

i.

Yesterday the river ice, till now page-blank, was annotated by coyotes. I followed their new year letters down along the west side of the island, a squat clay column crowned with sedge and hawthorn trees. The river's white parentheses now hold it as a thing apart (a garden closed, a fountain sealed) but I have seen it whelmed with flood. I haven't been here since a child—

but I remember how a hawthorn tree affords a kind of shelter, makes a fortified enclosure. The flood-water has decked its branches: trailing sedge like empty sleeves, its crown bears up the sibyl-husks of marah, manroot, bitter water. *Are you here, my intimate God?* The way leads out of the charmed enclosure, out of the garden, from the child, and back into the busy-ness of life.

I know it will not be forever
that the silence will agree
to bear me up: a thaw's predicted.
But for now come walk with me,
my friend, along this frozen river.

Season of vision and delay:
the time it takes the kings to travel,
or a letter to arrive,
or there to be at last a day

that was cold enough. I think of Richard—
as the mercury sinks in the mouth of another
season—I think of him watching the weather.

If I had your eyes, perhaps
I could better read these tracks—
the coyotes' new year letters
marked out on the river ice:
how they meander, double back
for no apparent reason, then
go on again, and how they mean
nothing, and are for no one's eyes.

ii.

That night when we were drinking at
the pub close by St Thomas's,
you lectured me about the *Phaedo:*

'The subject comes from the occasion,
not the other way around.'

Just so: I'd talk with you, my friend,
of orchards or tides or the alphabet—
but I must take the text I'm set,
by text and by our conversation,
by an accident of dates:
that asterisk, your small aside
re. Williams, *Eros crucified.*

Relational god, the word, my Eros,
god of the space- and time-abridging
arrows: how far can he carry
in the name of God, how much,
metapherein, mortal touch?

You've said you fear encountering him—
midway along the hall of this
our life, on your way to the bathroom at night,
or, *also in the evening, in*
an orchard partway down a row
between the apple trees. But whom?

The personage your fear encounters,
is it lover, father, son,
your friend, *somewhere beyond myself*
I wait for my arrival—
at the point you marked on maps
with an uncompleted asterisk,
in childhood, with a canted x?

I never knew what Auden meant
when he said he was a Christian because
there was no other god aroused
all sides of his being to the cry
'Crucify him'—

                    but it was I
who strung him up in the civic square
of myself, my Eros, sacker of cities,
god of love, disfigured statue.

Why am I surprised to find
him there?

iii.

You've said you feel a loss in letters:
it's in *the closeness of improvised
conversation* your mind comes alive—
that's Heighton's *winter room,
where the words resonate, wrestle,
and blend*....This in one of my favourite
poems about friendship. My friend,
what can survive the killing cold
of letters, then? The mooted choice,
either *strictly speaking, to silent
fall,* or to write: the crucified voice.

Child of the first, most painful divisions;
that in which the universe tries
to put itself back together again
and again and again and again and again—
Was ist deine leidendste Erfahrung?—
he became silence, he became distance.

I write small poems. They are more given
to the enfleshment of a vision
than to the sustenance of belief,
but I'll stretch this one out for you—
the first light of the universe,
hammered to the thickness of gold leaf.

iv.

The river's white parentheses—
that frozen torrent, roaring silence—
threaten the *logos* of the island.
All that's necessary strictly
is to silent fall, wrote Richard, *never*
to speake again. Outwintering me,
turning his bitter water to wine.

You asked me if I write for him
and I said I can't, because he's gone.

I was to see him in Port Hope
that winter but there was a thaw,
and rain, and then it all froze up
and he forbade me to attempt
the drive, and anything he would
have bid me then I would have done—
in fact did do: I told the phone
goodbye, went home by other ways,
and one month later he was dead.
You are among my loves, he said.

There is that sound beyond all language,
cry of all that's sad and strange,
coyotes howling, wynde and rayne.
I hear it sometimes too in poems,
in the perfection of the rhymes.

v.

God of my youth, returned to haunt
my middle age, reminding me
I promised him all kinds of things
when I was young and unavailed
of them—my heart, my firstborn child—
but what he wants is always something
other than what we volunteer.

'There will be no suffering here':
the world that knew I wouldn't face
the fact that there is no such place
has let me hear it in your voice.

vi.

Metapherein, mortal touch,
who made the gods ridiculous
with transformations—birds and beasts
and even, once, a human being—
so that at last they strung him up,
metapherein, mortal touch.

'*My Eros is crucified:* what does that mean?
My desire is transformed.'

Yes, but how? Redeemed? Disarmed?
Or given fresh artillery,
not the arrow but the way:

Sein Ausgang eilet aus der Höhe
in euer Mutter Haus....

vii.

This morning I can hear the wind:
it held its fire on the morning
I was walking on the river,
talking to you in my mind,
but right now it howls around
my study. I can hear it in
this poem, the loneliness of letters:
this although the poets say
before the word was sign or symbol,
sacrament, or flesh and blood,
it was this—what? This gap, this Love.

Wiman calls Christ 'contingency'.
What happens, to the God's what is.
Sometimes I pray to that what is—
to help me value, as you say,
the actual over the possible,
and over freedom, yes, the good:
O da quod jubes, Domine.

Meanwhile what happens picks its way
amid the matted river sedges,
in among the hawthorn branches,
out on the wide river ice,
accident and happenstance

20

and chance encounter and the glancing
blow: *Christ!* Can one pray to that?

viii.

On a westbound train to Union
Station I have just, like you,
reread Auden's *New Year Letter,*
thinking, Who could write a better?,
knowing that Himself now sits
upon the jury with the wits,
the metaphysicists, the liars,
the soothsayers, hanging fire
while I step onto the stand
who would presume to try my hand
at a verse letter to a friend
on the occasion of the end
of an old year or the beginning
of a new. What would he make of mine—
the poem as intimate aside,
all asterisk and otherwise—
who even in his lover's bed
prepared Dispatches to the Reader;
or me, who even on the stand
rehearses letters to a friend?

I hate to think. And yet his measure's
home to me. It gives me pleasure
just to hear it in my head,
after Auden's sense has fled:

those tidy couplets locked away
against the closing of the day,
each item summoned and, dismissed
by rhyme, checked off the list—
you see, my thoughts will neatly queue
for it; however, friend, for you,
I will lay down the weapon of the iamb:

Look, look there, on the exposed ascenders—
see the clumps of fleshgrass caught?
That's evidence of flooding.
                              Once,
the silent torrent whelmed the verses.

        ix.

Season of waiting, secret birth,
season of travel— Now we disperse,
to our own countries, by Other ways,
doubling back upon ourselves,
hiding our scent in the stench of the dead,
going cross-country, taking to water—
Zu dem raschen Wasser sprich:
What is it that is most bitter?

'It aches my heart,' you said, 'let's go.'

Yes, out of these cold exclosures
back to winter rooms—

(& still,
this feeling I sometimes have that all
that's necessary strictly is to silent
fall, to stay out in the wynde and rayne
until it turns to ice

       & snow—

beneficent, like that which fell
from heaven down into the streetlight
where I stood and raised my arms
up into it, an act of praise,
impulsively, after we parted,
turning to go our separate ways—
you down into St George Station,
I back to the library
where I'd been reading. You had placed
your hand just briefly on the back
of my hatless head as we embraced,
then let me go. Commands of Grace.

    x.

That such precise / Commands of Grace
Grow myriad / In time and place,
As Sacrament / Embodied there;
What more shall mortal / Body bear?

Thus Richard, who, when I resumed,
in somewhat less than sober state,
my carrel (pun intended), as

he sometimes does dispatched to me
(MS collection 4-5-7:
these the coordinates of heaven?)
what I needed—here it is,
the onlie ending of my poem:

Here we bring new water
　　from the well so clear,
For to worship God with,
　　this Happy New Year.

Sing levy dew, sing levy dew,
　　the water and the wine;
The seven bright gold wires
　　and the bugles that do shine.

Sing reign of Fair Maid
　　with gold upon her toe,—
Open you the West Door,
　　and turn the Old Year go.

Sing reign of Fair Maid
　　with gold upon her chin,—
Open you the East Door,
　　and let the New Year in.

Sing levy dew, sing levy dew,
　　the water and the wine;
The seven bright gold wires
　　and the bugles that do shine.

FINAL CORRESPONDENCE, ON A GALLERY NOTECARD
SHOWING A DETAIL FROM A MARGINAL DECORATION
IN THE LUTTRELL PSALTER

Still stricken by your glyph, I flip the card.
The Magi, on the verso, are engaged in conversation.
I rehearse again as they do
the significance of their gifts,
and thus we pass the hours of the journey:

gold, and frankincense, and myrrh; and gold,
and frankincense, and myrrh; and gold....

Richard, these roughshod pelters are unhurried—
but neither do they turn, and they have carried
all five of us a decade forth
in time from when you trusted this
to post, and look around us: there are children.

And he came by the Spirit into the temple: and when the parents brought
    in the child Jesus, to do for him after the custom of the law,
Then took he him up in his arms, and blessed God, and said,
Lord, now lettest thou thy servant depart in peace, according to thy word:
For mine eyes have seen thy salvation,
Which thou hast prepared before the face of all people;
A light to lighten the Gentiles, and the glory of thy people Israel.
And Joseph and his mother marvelled at those things which were
    spoken of him.
And Simeon blessed them, and said unto Mary his mother, Behold, this
    child is set for the fall and rising again of many in Israel; and for a
    sign which shall be spoken against;
(Yea, a sword shall pierce though thy own soul also,) that the thoughts
    of many hearts may be revealed.
    —Luke 2:27–35

Ich habe genug....ich habe den Heiland, das Hoffen der Frommen,
auf meine begierigen Arme genommen; ich habe genug....—Anon.

i. Te lucis ante terminum

Before the end we turn
to the beginning—morning,

origin—entrust
ourselves to that, replacing

light for darkness in our inner
eye: poet, beginner,

who can say how far
down into the night we are

able to transport
that guttered flame?

ii. Annunciation

Nothing asked me
to keep mum:
how could nothing,
being dumb,

put the question—
not to say
present it as
accomplished *fait*.

Nobody asked me
and I heard
and I answered:
flesh, word.

iii. Conception

Everything beyond the dock
was a bright void, as if the far
shore had not been thought of yet,

then a whet of sun revealed
the silken rumple of the water.
I was with child by everything when we met.

iv. Advice

I wanted to talk with you about
the child that openeth the womb,
the sword that openeth the wound,
the word that openeth the mouth—

> *Behold, this child*
> *is set for the fall*
> *and rising again*
> *of many in Israel;*

> *and for a sign*
> *which shall be spoken*
> *against; (Yea,*
> *a sword shall pierce*

> *through thy own soul*
> *also,) that the thoughts*
> *of many hearts*
> *may be revealed—*

but you were pierced, and thought about
the word that openeth the wound,
the sword that openeth the womb,
the child that openeth his mouth.

v. It Is Enough

It is enough
to know that my
redeemer lieth
in my arms.

*

Four things say not
it is enough:
the grave, the womb,
the earth, and fire.

*

Though not so deep
as a well, nor wide,
it is enough,
'twill serve, I'm peppered.

*

That love is all
there is is all
we know of love.
It is enough.

vi. The Temple

Now let me go according to thy word.
You said I should not see the end until
I'd seen the beginning: here it is, here
it is, I've held it in my arms, the light,
now let me go according to thy word.

The thoughts of many hearts shall be revealed,
you said. I kept those sayings in my heart,
a sword to pierce me: here it is, here
it is, I've held it in my arms, the night.
The thoughts of many hearts shall be revealed.

vii. Senex puerum portabat / Lullaby

Father you carry, held up by
the child that you carry, the child
born to a child whose child-
hood even childbirth couldn't smother,
who loved her newborn baby like a father.

It's okay you can go now, I am holding you,
you thought you had so very far to go, but you are home now.

viii. Birth

The darkness doesn't
fathom light,
the sea the land,
or death, life,

but out of the other
comes the one.
The sea delivers
up the sun,

the sea delivers
up the sun,
the sea delivers
up the sun.

THE LIFE TO COME

Easy to follow
you in, who'd show
me nothing that wasn't
there. The high
hard country
of the vaulted
ceiling where
the light comes through
uncoloured glass,
the way the way
declines from here
to *euer Mutter Haus.*

*

Your handwriting
reminded me
of snowfencing
on rural roads,
tenaciously canted
in the effort
of just staying
where it is
so that the silence
is allowed
to mass along
the leeward side.

*

To find the high,
hard places in
the country that
I come from is
to stand on a level
while the river
eats it away
before your feet:
then the wild
geese lift from the water—
dark on their backs,
all bright beneath.

*

I think about
rugosa roses,
wild, unruly,
no-one-planted,
barrier and passage-
way, their bay-
wind-beaten
strange embraces
offering neither
stem nor stalk,
not at all
that can be gathered

EVEN SO I'LL GATHER ROSES
after Ich will doch wohl Rosen brechen *(Bach)*

Even so I'll gather roses,
careless of the piercing thorns—
though a thorn should be a sword—
confident my supplications
pierce the heart of my creator,
who has given me his word.

Even though a sword should pierce
through my own soul I would come here,
gathering as I've always done
roses in the giant's garden,
in the garden of the lord
who has given me his son.

EROS AND PSYCHE

The lights went on
and instantly

I saw it: you,
immortal; I,

consigned to any
trial your mother

might devise
(beans, rice,

golden fleece
in the thorn tree,

pick-up Styx):
the end—if not

that in that lightning-
bolted instant

you saw it: me,
immortal; you,

consigned to any
trial my mother

might devise.

PSYCHE

I got myself
in trouble with
a god back there,

persisting in
my folly, hoping
graceful error

might correct
the cave, a grazing
arrow give

a shape to airy
nothing, illicit
light to shiftless

Eros a local
habitation
and a name.

…it is impossible to read some of the documents, La Vita Nuova,
for example, many of Shakespeare's sonnets or the Symposium
and dismiss them as fakes. —W. H. Auden

It is not given one to follow
into another's heaven or hell.
Neither conclusively, female nor male.

Endless means, prolific dearth.
I have this one name I can call you.
That's what the documents say. For what they're worth.

Water, they say,
is taught by thirst:
thirst has worn
the path that winds
uphill to the well
where I went, as I thought,

for my water and where
I met you first—
I met you there
and now I know
that thirst is also
taught by water.

MORE STANZAS FOR SIMEON

It is enough, it will suffice:
I took him in my arms. He was
an image of the life to come.

Now lettest thou thy servant
depart in peace, I thought.
And thought of the dying words of Keats:

Severn, lift me up, for I
am dying. I shall die easy. Don't
be frightened. Thank God it has come.

It had not come. For seven
hours more Keats fought
for breath in that Italian room.

Good woman, take heaven back:
I've held it in my arms but I
am powerless to comfort it.

FIRE FLOWER
after Rosemary Kilbourn

And all shall be well, and all shall be well, and all manner
of thing shall be well. — Julian of Norwich

    i.

These lines a cage that lions you,
around, all through the bars of which
you fall upon me still, as light.
      Expect another, longer letter soon.

    ii.

Here, where I have wounded wood
and forthwith came there out March light,
I walk to see whom I have pierced.
      Expect another, longer letter soon.

    iii.

My palimpsested lines occlude you:
could ungraving them reveal you,
or would you vanish utterly then?
      Expect another, longer letter soon.

iv.

My lines insist upon what is:
you stalk me in the hill's green gestures,
saying, *Deare hart, how like you this?*
        Expect another, longer letter soon.

v.

Since I've been out walking here
the sun has risen, present perfect.
Sun rose, in the simple past,
        a fire flower. Where are you?

vi.

Expect another, longer letter soon.

A SUGAR BUSH IN HOLY WEEK

In the amitie I speak of, they entermixe and confound
themselves one in the other, with so universall a commixture,
that they weare out, and can no more finde the seme that hath
conjoyned them together. — Michel de Montaigne

that if our shadows rise up like
Charlier's apostles, they might at least
cast on the ground where they have so
long lain, the forest floor regreening
as if it were at last spring, light

      *

that there prove sufficient summers'
growth in these regreening trees
to brook the Christ-side-piercing spear
of prayer for honey in the mouth
of death (or was it life? or was it spring?)

      *

that walking amid the risen light
I might confound my shadow in
these tree shadows so utterly
that I weare out, can no more finde,
the seme that hath conjoyned us together

i. Le Jeudy Saint
after Delalande

　　Aleph.

Let us bring our grief to numbers—
like a cloth spread on a table;
like a table of unfinished
board; or like a cloth the blue
of chicory; or like a *Lamed*
placed, a cup upon a table—
et videte si est dolor
si est dolor sicut dolor
dolor sicut dolor meus…

　　Aleph.

Are there syllables in English
capable of this soprano
voice that's singing out its heart
in lamentation, I mean Latin—
me minavit et adduxit
in tenebris, non in lucem—

breaking in these Hebrew letters
in the darkness where you lead me,
aleph, aleph, aleph, beth?

   Aleph.

There was never grief like hers:
in all the mornings into which
the sun arose, improbably,
uncomprehended differently
by every day in all the evenings
into which it fell, *a fleshstone*
from the topmast / crosstree; and
in all the nights, no grief like hers.
And none like mine. And none like yours.

ii. Le Vendredy Saint

There is the dark that falls upon.
There is the dark that lies upon.
There is the dark that lies in wait.

There is the dark that doesn't lie
in wait but simply waits, attendant,
on the waters' face before

the names exist for day and night.
For what is it waiting, this attendant
dark, in which I find myself

awake? Wake up, explain again,
to my tenebrae, your light.

iii. Le Samedy Saint

Over here, no sight, no sound,
no smell, no taste, no touch, I wake,
a smaller darkness opening onto darkness,

and yet whose voice, if I awake,
but yours whose voice you say is calling
from the heights to wake me so

I will not miss your call, calls me
awake; whose light, if I arise,
but yours whose light you say is dawning

there to bid me rise so I
won't miss your dawn, bids me arise?

A POOR PASSION
after Bach's Johannes-Passion

*'Arise, my love, my beautiful one and come away...' These words are the
luminous mystery hidden in the cry from the Cross, 'My God, My God,
why hast thou forsaken me?'* —Christopher Snook

i. Denn es war kalt
It is early morning: so early it is dark; the scene, an outer courtyard
in the palace of the high priest. Servants and officers of the high
priest are standing about; perhaps somebody's dog is here; there's
the person who minds the door.... Another person is here, as well:
it's Simon Peter, and his heart is troubled in him, for his beloved
Master, his teacher, has been arrested, and even now is being
questioned by the high priest. Simon Peter has gained entry to the
palace thanks to the offices of another of the teacher's disciples, but
now that he is inside, among the servants of the household—
among the soldiers, these armed men—he finds himself denying
his acquaintance with the teacher: a necessary fiction, he tells
himself, one that will allow him to remain undetected here; perhaps
to help, in some way. When it really matters, he tells himself, he
will cast off the cloak of dissimulation. But for now—well, for now
he'll step a little closer to the fire. It is a fire of coals, and these
people—the people of the house; the people mostly nameless in
this story—have made it. They stand about the fire warming
themselves.

It is a passing moment in the Gospel of John, practically a
parenthetical insertion, and yet, in Bach's setting of the John

Passion, his *Johannes-Passion*, the Evangelist lingers over this moment: 'It was cold,' he tells us. *Denn es war kalt.* It is what Robert Creeley might call 'the instant of the one humanness' in Bach's plan of it. Yes, friends, lovers, brothers, sisters … :
it is cold.

It's cold. We draw a little nearer to the fire. In Mi'kma'ki, where I write this, Sacred Fires have been lit and tended for thousands of years. I stood beside one on the waterfront three days ago, warming my hands like Simon Peter, at a flame that was, to misremember Wallace Stevens, not myself and much more not my own.

European settlers in this region—I am one more wave—brought with them their plagues and their stories. In one of these stories, fire is symbolic of the Holy Ghost or Spirit, the Comforter: the breath of storytelling in community, which comes to reconcile us to our losses, to revivify our spirits, and/or to guide us deeper into hope—to encourage and inspire us after we have been forsaken. Only after we have been forsaken, we are told, will this Spirit come.

In the hands of power, stories become plagues: they are wielded as doctrine, and used to repress, to silence, to assimilate and destroy. But I don't think stories are happy there, in the hands of power; I think the holy spirit, the inspiring voice, deserts stories so conscripted. It goes back to the root of breath, the sacred fire, to inspire another teller, another version—to enter the world again, as life and light.

ii. New Wine in Old Bottles
I am not the first poet-translator, in English or otherwise, to offer up new words for Bach's *Johannes-Passion*. There is a long tradition of

this kind of work, which musicologists sometimes call *contrafactum*—a kind of *poeisis* 'whereby the music is retained and the words altered' (OED). Common in medieval and Renaissance music, the practice is still with us in folk song and in hymnody—and of course in childhood: ask any six-year-old who has gleefully chanted, *Joy to the world, the school burned down*.... The practice of contrafactum has analogies in written verse (think of stanzaic poetry) and in life. (What am I, post-transition, but an old tune with new lyrics?)

A counterfeiter (a maker of *contrafacta*) may be a translator, his work impelled by a felt sense of the affective charge that comes with experiencing a great work of vocal music—singing it and/or hearing it—in one's own vernacular. And/or, he may be a poet, looking to speak back to the original text, in ways obvious or subtle, by adopting its form. Contrafacta have often been used—slyly, reverently, or both—to introduce secular material into sacred contexts, and vice versa; contrafactum is thus a technology (ancient, simple, and marvellously complex) through which, as Richard Outram puts it, 'once, again, / The sacred [is] proved / By the profane.' (The words appear in his beautiful poem 'Eros Incarnate.')

Daniel Cabena, my dear friend and co-conspirator, who proposed to me the project of this Passionate retelling, tells me that contrafactum is often explained as 'the practice of pouring new wine into old bottles.' *Don't* pour new wine into old bottles, we are cautioned in the Gospels—but notably not in John. I like to think that John was a poet. As a poet, he might have known, with Richard Wilbur, that when you pour new wine into old bottles, 'the bottles become new, too.'

My contrafactum is a new bringing-over, into Bach's music, of the Passion story. My principal source is Bach's libretto: I am indebted to Pamela Dellal's literal translation of it, which was published on line by Emmanuel Music; and also to the 2004 Channel-Classics recording of the *Johannes-Passion* by the Netherlands Bach Society, whose musical gestures I have followed. Just as Bach did, however, I have allowed myself to draw on a wide range of 'sacred poems and private ejaculations' (to use George Herbert's phrase), in my libretto-making (and in particular in the [re]making of the arias and chorales): Passion versions that are significant to me and/ or that are part of the history of this story in my mother-tongue. Readers will hear echoes of the John and Matthew Passions from the King James Version of the Bible, of the Coverdale Psalms and the Book of Common Prayer, of fairy stories, hymns, vernacular poetry, private life....

What moved me about Bach's *Johannes-Passion* when I first heard it—what continues to move me about it—is the way the arias and chorales bloom up in the midst of the Evangelist's narrative, small queer love songs, in the desert of his passionate recitative.

iii. What Manner of Man
Though Christianity grew up as a religion along with the written word, and in some ways functions as a meditation upon the written word, in the medium of the written word, Bach's version of the Saint John Passion is very much in an oral tradition also. First of all, it is made to be sung. Music is a close sister of memory; words set to music become memorable words; singers and parishioners know by heart, in their bones and their blood, the Saint John Passion in Bach's setting. And then, too, Bach's *Johannes-Passion* begins with an almost bardic invocation of the muse—or

of God; or, of his Son (the mythos calls us to experience identity here):

Herr, unser Herrscher, dessen Ruhm
In allen Landen herrlich ist!
  Zeig uns durch deine Passion,
  Daß du, der wahre Gottessohn,
  Zu aller Zeit,
  Auch in der größten Niedrigkeit,
  Verherrlicht worden bist!

God, our God, renowned in every land! Show us how through your Passion you, the true Son of God, have—through all time, and even in the greatest humiliation—become transfigured.

It is an invocation of God, as I have said. But the one who steps in to tell the story to *us*—this strange story, in which God the Father becomes the Son of God, in which passion is humiliation and humiliation is transfiguration (what a transition!)—is the storyteller, the Evangelist. (The word, at root, means 'bringer of good tidings'; it should not be confused with 'Proselytist'.) Hearing, he tells.

My Evangelist is a storyteller. Perhaps he is a travelling person: a person who, as in Psalm 84, the beautiful *Quam dilecta*, carries 'in his heart…the pilgrim ways.' Perhaps his friend, a musician, travels with him. Perhaps they live in time of plague, and have been forced to flee their home community. Perhaps they flee the fallout of a love, that Passion the story of which the Evangelist carries with him, a burden and a light. My Evangelist is a German speaker: the version of the Passion that he knows is the one that's in the

Luther Bible, the one Bach used in his setting—a setting the Evangelist knows too, in his bones and his blood, because he is not only a storyteller; he is a singer.

Perhaps it is winter; at any rate, it is ... *kalt*. He comes upon some other travellers. They are gathered about a fire. The storyteller and his musician friend draw nearer. They warm themselves. Eventually, these travellers—who are they? sinners? saints?—ask the question, the great, original question: *My God, my God, why hast thou forsaken me?*

And then they ask the other great, original question: *Will you tell us a story?*

I imagine the Passion acted, sung, and played by a small company of performers, with minimal staging: a 'Poor Passion', in the Grotowskian sense. It is in the round. There is no strict barrier, physical or actual, between the performers and the audience. The instrumentation need not at all be Bach's. Some of the italicized sections below that are chorales in the original may become solos, if the company desires. Arias may be transposed for voice-types other than those Bach's original prescribes. For reasons of allowing maximal openness here, none of the italicized sections below are attributed to particular characters or groups of characters: they are free for the taking, by whomever is moved to sing or say them.

Sometimes, the performers are the audience for the storyteller's tale; sometimes, they help him perform it, as he invites or appoints them, and/or as they themselves are inspired to interrupt and/or join in. They assume various roles within the story—and sometimes they speak from their hearts, as themselves (and in so doing draw on the Passion versions, sacred and secular, holy and profane, that are familiar to them). It is a story that lives in the telling.

This story is serious, but it is also funny. The teller is passionate (these are the most important things that have ever happened to him), but he is not above sending up the pompous priests, the unctuously self-righteous crowd, and he enjoys inviting his interlocutors to join with him in this sport. He is not without a conscience, however: he understands that he, too, has crucified his true love at Golgotha.

He is a virtuoso, able to translate the Luther John Passion on the fly, in meet syllabics, into a language not his own—though his diction and syntax are occasionally strained in the doing. It is the English of a second-language speaker: the fingerprints of the German are still on it (just as the fingerprints of the Greek were still on Luther's German, as they are on the English of the King James Version). But more important to the Evangelist than fluency, than mastering the English idiom, is that he convey something of the motion of meaning in the music. And he trusts that what his interlocutors will hear, here—what they will translate into their own hearts' knowledge and speak back to him in all their own hearts' languages—is the truth: that radiant entity which, in this moment, it has been given him to serve, in the joy of his craft, with the inspiration of the Holy Spirit, without fear.

My Evangelist is a storyteller; he is a human being. He is not necessarily a he.

They are a person in love.

PART ONE

Lord! O, my God, why have you—
have you forsaken me, my God?
Tell me again the story
where you, forsaken by my God,
become like me,
changing the face of agony
into the face of love.

Evangelist Jesus went with his disciples over the brook Cedron—
there was a garden—to rest there—Jesus and his disciples. Judas,
however, who would betray him, knew of the place too, for
Jesus had often before gone there with his disciples. So then
Judas, who'd assembled a party of men, with the chief priests'
and the Pharisees' permission, came to the place, with torches,
lanterns, and with weapons. And so Jesus, who foresaw this,
all that would come upon him, went out to meet them and
addressed them:

Jesus Whom do you seek?

Evangelist They responded to him,

Chorus Jesus of Nazareth, Jesus of Nazareth.

Evangelist Jesus said to them,

Jesus I'm he.

Evangelist Judas also, his former friend, was standing with them. And when Jesus replied to them, 'I'm he,' then they all drew back and fell on their faces. He said to them a second time,

Jesus Whom do you seek?

Evangelist Again they said it:

Chorus Jesus, Jesus, Jesus of Nazareth.

Evangelist Then again he said it:

Jesus I'll tell you again that I'm he; since it's me you seek, take me and leave these others.

> *O holy love, O love beyond all measure*
> *that led you to this via dolorosa!*
> *The pleasure and the joy were mine, Beloved,*
> *and yours the sorrow.*

Evangelist And thus the saying was fulfilled, the words he had spoken: 'The ones you gave into my keeping, not one of them shall be taken.' But Simon Peter having a sword, he took it out, and struck at the servant of the priest, and took his whole right ear off. (Yes, Sir, that was Malchus.) Then said Jesus to Peter,

Jesus Put up your sword and be quiet. The cup my father's given to me, shall I not drink it? The cup my father's given, shall I not drink it?

> *The cup that you have given me—*
> *O how can I refuse it?*

You taught me that to keep my life
I must prepare to lose it.
Now Father glorify thy Son:
teach me to pray, Thy will be done.

Evangelist The band of men and the overseer, all the party of
Judas, handcuffed Jesus, arrested him, paraded him directly to
Hannas, who was kinsman to Caiaphas—Caiaphas, the one who
was the high priest that year. Remember that Caiaphas had
advised the council that it was good that one man should be
sacrificed for all.

To release me from the bondage
of my unlikeness,
so my God is taken,
and my God is godforsaken:
made in my likeness,
broken in my breaking.

Evangelist Simon Peter though, he followed along with them,
and so did one other.

I follow you likewise: it is no journey.
I cannot forsake
my life and my light.
The burden is light
and easy the yoke:
continue to guide me, to move me, to turn me.

Evangelist The other disciple was already known to the priest, and
followed Jesus right in to this priest's, the high priest's, dwelling.

Simon Peter stood outside by the door. And so the other disciple, whom the high priest knew just a little, went out, and argued a bit with the doorkeeper, and made her let Peter inside. Then said the woman, the doorkeeper, to Peter,

Woman Are you not one of those who were with Jesus?

Evangelist He said,

Peter I am not.

Evangelist And standing there were the soldiers and servants, and they had a coal fire lit, for it was cold. And warming himself, Simon Peter stood there with them, right there in their midst. Meanwhile the high priest was asking Jesus of his disciples and of his ideas. Jesus responded to him:

Jesus What I have said, all of it I put before the world. I've always openly instructed in the schools and in the temples, where every person could hear me speaking. What I have done, it was never in secret. Why question me about this? Go and ask the ones who, when I was teaching, were there to listen, what I have told them. Ask them: for they understand all the things I said unto them.

Evangelist Then, however, as he said this, one of those attending, a servant, struck him, right here on the cheek like this, and said,

Servant Are you mocking the high priest with these answers?

Evangelist Jesus spoke then directly to him:

Jesus Have I spoken amiss? Then correct me and I will mend my words. But if I have spoken well, why do you strike me?

> *O who hath dared to wound thee,*
> *my friend, the one who found me,*
> *what are these scars you have?*
> *Who is it that betrayed you?*
> *Tell me that I may slay them.*
> Nay, nay, these are the wounds of love.
>
> *Have I been so unkindly?*
> *The spring itself has shunned me.*
> *There is no blossoming.*
> *I am the one who left you;*
> *now I must bend to lift you*
> *into the branches of the tree.*

Evangelist Then Hannas sent him off in shackles to the high priest, Caiaphas. Simon Peter stood and warmed his hands. And then they said to him,

Chorus Are you not one of his disciples?

Evangelist He lowered his eyes and said,

Peter I am not.

Evangelist But another of the servants, a friend of him whom Peter had struck, wouldn't drop the subject:

Servant Weren't you one of those in the garden with him?

Evangelist A third time then Peter denied it. And then he heard it: the cock crew. Then recalling to himself the words of Jesus, he left the house, and cried the most bitter tears.

O, my sin.
Now who will take me in?
Where shall I find redemption?
Must I stay?
Can I go away
where my name is never mentioned?

You will leave what you hold dear;
learn the savour
of the bitter,
unfamiliar bread,
be the one who treads another's stair.

        *

Peter who gainsaid the Lord
when his courage failed him
with his better heart restored
bitterly bewailed him.

Jesus, turn your gaze on me,
calcine my unkindness;
when I disavow your love,
let me be reminded.

PART TWO

Where is your beloved gone,
fairest among women?
He is taken in the night,
like a common sinner.

In the streets I sought for you
but the watchmen found me
and my veil was torn in two
and they struck and wounded me.

Evangelist By then they had brought Jesus to Caiaphas in the courthouse. And it was early. But they didn't go in the courthouse: the Passover was upon them, and they wanted to partake of it. Then Pontius Pilate came out of the house and said,

Pilate What charges do you lay against this man?

Evangelist The whole company responded to him:

Chorus If indeed he were no evildoer, we wouldn't bring him here shackled before you.

Evangelist Then Pontius Pilate said to them,

Pilate Then take the man away, and judge of him according to your law.

Evangelist Then they all said to him,

Chorus We may not pass the sentence.

Evangelist And so it was fulfilled, the thing Jesus, earlier, said—when he prophesied how his death would come upon him. Then Pontius Pilate went back inside, in the courthouse, and called Jesus, and spoke to him:

Pilate Are you these people's king then?

Evangelist Jesus responded,

Jesus Do you say this thing yourself? Or is it that others have said this thing?

Evangelist Pilate then answered him:

Pilate Am I these people? It's them and the high priests who have brought these charges against you. What have you proclaimed?

Evangelist Jesus responded then:

Jesus My kingdom isn't of this world. If I were a king in this, your world, my disciples would have fought against you, so I would not have been taken captive and brought here—ah, but you see my kingdom isn't like that.

> *My kingdom isn't of this world, you told him.*
> *What use have you for frankincense or gold, then?*
> *What is there in my wretched heart to give you?*
> *How can I serve you?*

Love took my hand and smiling did reply,
who is it made that heart of yours but I?
'You must sit down,' says Love, 'and taste my meat.'
So I did sit and eat.

Evangelist Then said the governor to him,

Pilate So are you really a king then?

Evangelist Jesus answered him,

Jesus You say that I'm a king. The thing that I was born for, and came to the world for, is to bear witness to the truth. Whoever hears the truth, that person hears me speaking.

Evangelist Pontius Pilate then said,

Pilate What is truth then?

Evangelist And when he had so spoken, he went out and announced to the people—he said to them,

Pilate I cannot find the fault in him. You have, I know, a law that I may release to you a prisoner. What do you say, shall we let the Jewish king be set free then?

Evangelist The people together hollered out, and they said,

Chorus Not that one. Make it Barrabas.

Evangelist Barrabas, he was in for murder. Well now Pilate took Jesus and let him be scourged then.

> *My spirit, don't turn away: remember your affliction,*
> *your misery, the wormwood, and the gall.*
> *In your remembrance keep them, still.*
> *Recall them. Be humbled. There is hope here.*
> *The rowanberry flowers are blooming;*
> *you know their bitter fruit. It's good in a dry season.*
> *My spirit, don't turn away from him.*

*

> *Remember how the morning light was falling*
> *upon his shoulders:*
> *it was a sign of grace—*
> *the way after the night was over,*
> *there by your window he stood watching*
> *the light returning to the city—*
> *although you couldn't see his face.*

Evangelist And the company they plaited then a crown of thorns, and set it upon his head, and someone got a purple robe, and mocked him:

Chorus Hail to thee, O mighty King.

Evangelist And then once again they struck him. Then Pontius Pilate went back out, and spoke to the people:

Pilate See him, the way I'm going to bring him out—and understand it, that I cannot say he is guilty.

Evangelist And so they brought Jesus out, behold, in his thorny crown and his purple mantle. Pilate said to them,

Pilate See him. *Ecce homo.*

Evangelist But when the high priests and the servants saw him, straight away they hollered,

Chorus Crucify him, crucify him.

Evangelist Then Pilate said to them,

Pilate You can do this thing and crucify him, but know that I couldn't find him guilty.

Evangelist The people responded to him:

Chorus You know we have a law, and under this law we shall kill him, for he's made himself to be the Son of God.

Evangelist Now when Pilate had heard this, it worried him still more, and returning inside, to the courthouse, he said to Jesus,

Pilate Where did you come from?

Evangelist But now Jesus wouldn't give an answer. Desperate, Pilate went on:

Pilate Why won't you speak with me? Aren't you aware I have power that could crucify—and power too that could give pardon?

Evangelist Jesus now spoke to him:

Jesus The power that you have wouldn't be, if it were not given by my father who is in heaven. The others, who gave me over into your hands, theirs is the greater burden.

Evangelist From this time Pilate's only thought was how he might release him.

> *Our freedom when it comes to us*
> *will come through this captivity:*
> *our prison is a garden closed,*
> *our agony a fountain sealed,*
> *if we do not agree to bleed*
> *our wounds forever go unhealed.*

Evangelist The people, though, they clamoured, and told him,

Chorus If you let this Jesus go, you are not a friend of Caesar's. Calls himself a king, as if saying that he is greater than Caesar.

Evangelist Now when Pilate had heard all of this, then he brought Jesus back out, and readied himself for judgment in the place that, well we call it *Hochpflaster*. In the Hebrew though it's *Gabbatha*. It was now on the eve of the Passover, just about at midday, and he said to the people:

Pilate See him. This is your king.

Evangelist They hollered at him,

Chorus Away with him, crucify him!

Evangelist Pilate pleaded with them:

Pilate Shall I really crucify your king?

Evangelist The high priests now responded:

Chorus Ours? Ours? We have no king but Caesar, none but Caesar.

Evangelist So then he gave in to them, and said that they might crucify Jesus. They fell upon him, Jesus, and hurried him away. And he bore his cross. They took him to the place that, we call it *Schädelstätt*, but they call it in the Hebrew *Golgotha*.

> Come, who would true valour see,
> *Come, O sinner, come with me.*
> *Come—O where—Jerusalem.*
>
> Bring your arrows of desire,
> *bring—O where—refining fire.*
> *Bring it to Jerusalem.*

Evangelist And they crucified him there, and with him two other ones, there by his side, Jesus right there in the midst of them. Then Pilate took a plank and he wrote on it, and set it upon the cross, and what it said was, 'Jesus of Nazareth, your God and King.' And these words of his, everyone read them, for the city was close by that place, where Jesus was crucified. And the words were written in the Hebrew, German, and the English language. Then all the high priests of the people said to Pilate,

Chorus Do not write 'your God and King,' rather that he laid claim to this: 'I am your God and King.'

Evangelist But Pilate responded:

Pilate The words that I have written—they are the words I've written.

> *The way across all space*
> *and time you came to me,*
> *revealing in your grace*
> *my soul's captivity;*

> *the gentle way you saw me*
> *when I was suffering*
> *and took my cross upon you:*
> *it is enough for me.*

Evangelist The executioners, those four soldiers who'd crucified Jesus, took away his clothing and divvied it up, in a way that each soldier kept some for himself. Same thing with the robe. The robe, however, was one cloth, from top to bottom woven seamlessly. So then they said one to another,

Chorus Let us cast lots for it, all of us doing it, and see who wins.

Evangelist And so it was fulfilled, the scripture that predicted 'They've divvied up my clothing all among themselves, and they have also, for my robe, cast lots among them.' This is what the soldiers did. But standing there by the cross was Mary, Jesus' mother; and Jesus' mother's sister, that Mary, Cleophas' wife; also Mary of Magdala. And now Jesus, when he saw his mother, and there also that disciple that—his beloved—said these words to his mother:

Jesus Mother, see him: this is your son.

Evangelist And addressing his disciple:

Jesus See her: this is she, your mother.

> *Mother now behold your son,*
> *son behold your mother;*
> *lover now behold your love,*
> *love behold your lover.*
>
> *O you, absolute for death,*
> *following behind me:*
> *if you love me feed my sheep,*
> *tarry till I find thee.*

Evangelist And thereafter, they cared for one another. And then, for Jesus knew that almost all was accomplished, so the word would be made truthful he cried out:

Jesus I'm thirsty.

Evangelist Some vinegar stood in a flask there. And somebody had a kind of sponge, and soaked it, and lashed it to a stalk of hyssop, and using this reached up to Jesus. And when Jesus had drunk what he could from the hyssop, he said,

Jesus His will is done.

> *His will is done:*
> *O rest for the unresting spirit.*
> *The forecast storm*
> *has spent itself upon the seawall.*
> *The agony is over now.*
> *It is enough.*
> *His will is done.*

Evangelist He lowered his head and departed.

> *My sweet redeemer let me ask you—*
> *O can you hear me from the scaffold? Up there on the scaffold?*
> *You said yourself 'His will is done.'*
> *Have you by this redeemed my sin? Have you redeemed my sin?*
> *Is your appalling death the face*
> *of prophesied salvation?*
> *Is all the world recovered here?*
> *My comforter is comfortless—O are you comfortless?—*
> *and yet your lowered head, your head,*
> *is clear. Its silent 'yes'.*

*

One thing only I desire,
one thing I require:
even this, that I should dwell
in thy habitation,

that I may behold thy face
in thy new creation,
with thee in thy dwelling place,
God of my salvation.

Evangelist And the veil of the temple was torn then in two, like this, and the sky went dark.

Break heart, I prithee break, my heart—
the one who fashioned earth and heaven
is growing cold. What have I done?
That I should live, and heaven's son
give up the ghost. He's gone for ever.
Dissolve, my spirit. Never, never—
O will you never come again?

*

Unfeeling creation, unfasten the river
and let it brim over.
Now tell this to everyone under the sun:
your Jesus is gone.

Evangelist And now the people, for it was the Sabbath eve, so that the corpses would not stay up there on the crosses till

morning (this particular Sabbath day was so great), counselled
Pontius Pilate to let their legs be broken and to have them taken
down then. So duly the soldiers went over, and broke then the legs
of the first one, and the second too, the others crucified there.
When however they came to Jesus, and they saw it, that he had
already died, they didn't do the same to him. One of the soldiers
however thrust thus into Jesus' torso, he used his spear, and
springing forth came blood and also water. And he who has seen
this has told it to you now, and his witness is true—and he telling
it knows, that where the truth is spoken, you will believe it. For
all of these things happened, so that the word would be made
truthful: 'You shall not break a bone of Jesus'—and also another
saying that goes, 'They will behold him: they will behold whom
they have pierced.'

> ...in the night he was betrayed
> took the Bread and brake it,
> after he had given thanks,
> bade them take and eat it...

> *You who made the water wine*
> *back at the beginning*
> *that I might believe on you,*
> *teach me now to drink it.*

Evangelist And now to Pilate came Joseph of Arimathaea, one
of Jesus' followers, in secret, fearing the people, and he asked him
if he could take Jesus' body. And so Pilate permitted it. And also
then came Nicodemus, the one who in the night had come to
Jesus once, and he brought myrrh, and aloe, a fragrant mixture,

a hundred pounds' worth. They brought away the corpse of Jesus,
and swaddled it in linen scented with myrrh and aloe, in the
Jewish style of preparation. Not far away from Golgotha, nearby
the crucifix, was a garden, and within it a new grave, a grave
where nobody had lain before. In this grave Jesus was laid,
then—it was as the people desired—upon the Sabbath evening.

> *Go well. I'm laying you my weeping.*
> *I feel it now: you are not leaving.*
> *Go well. Soon comes the break of day.*
> *And God shall wipe away all tears:*
> *there shall be neither pain nor fear*
> *nor sorrow, for the former things are passed away.*

*

> *The roses are in bloom again*
> *above the place where I slip in*
> *and leave my worldskins on the shore.*
> *The swallows go amid the wind*
> *and damselflies, and trout abound*
> *here where there were no trout before:*

> *O let me be a part of this!*
> *How lovely is thy dwelling place,*
> *O Lord of hosts, the swallow's rest,*
> *the sparrow's food. My heart and flesh*
> *rejoice in thee, O living god, O Jesus Christ.*
> Praise ye the Lord. / Thy Name be praised.

when at last the stone was rolled back
from the heart the tomb was empty
and she wept who would have kissed
even that instrument of torture
which had been the last to lift him

           I would kiss her body
              were she body.

           I would kiss her bones
              were they not ash.

           I would kiss her ashes
              but they are scattered.

           Last night last night
              she kissed me last…

at your chest the water cut you
where your body cut the water
line the line your arm extended
proffering the wet uncoupled
damselfly your love had rescued

WHICH IS THE CANTUS FIRMUS, DAN?

The waves' rote, or the rocks' withdrawing
sizzle—or is it the man
who sits and sings on a rock in the sun,
completely unprepared for how

the *contratenor* surfaces
and swims along for a measure, more,
above the bluegreen *superius*
before burying itself like a thread, a seal—

& then the woodwinds shriek like gulls
whose courses cross each other, still
the ocean's *tenor* holding, and—
I find that I've stopped singing. Dan,

if I can't yet sustain this glory,
it's enough to know you can.

BALLAD
after David Thomson

I was well past child-bearing years
and children had, though only three,
when I was walking on the strand
and a sea-grey selkie said to me,

> *O come away, my beautiful one,*
> *arise and come away with me.*
> *I am a man upon the land,*
> *I am a selkie in the sea.*

O how can I away with you?
A man I have, and children three.
If you had come when I was young
I would have gone away with thee.

> And home I went to my husband true
> and bounced my babies on my knee,
> but my dreams were full of the selkie's song,
> and the *Eli, Eli* of the sea.

So I went down to the shore again
and said, *All right, I'll go with thee:*
come up and claim what is thine own.
No answer came from the seal-grey sea.

So I went home to my husband true
and sang to my beautiful children three,
I am a woman on the land,
I am a selkie in the sea.

O come away, my beautiful one.
O why hast thou forsaken me?

CAENEUS

and the sea went over
or the girl went under
hard to know whichever
and the sound

begging him to change her
to a boy forever
so they all would know that
she had drowned

could have been her voice it
could have been the waves though
could have been his voice it
could have been the waves though

LULLABY

The wind blows where
it listeth the bank
swallows out to sea,
they return to the cliff face.

Foxhole, bird's nest, where you lay your head my breast.

The earth lets slip
its fox kits to go
mousing in the field,
they'll return here by darkness.

Foxhole, bird's nest, where you lay your head my breast.

DEUS EST SPHAERA CUJUS CENTRUM UBIQUE
CIRCUMFERENTIA NULLIBI
after Nymphes nappés *(des Prez) and Kathleen Raine*

Nereids, dryads, hamadryads: your daughter,
come mourn for her—for she can mourn no more.
I tried my best to serve the love I bore,
and my delight is turning back to water.

    *

For you have married me with rings of water,
with bright rings, whose ripples
circumference your sea.

AND TOOK HER BY THE HAND, AND CALLED,

SAYING, MAID, ARISE

we came out on a road between a field
which was the sea incarnate on the land

its grasses allatonce bothatonce coming and going,
which is to be understanding of the wind

which is to magnify the wind its turnings
in sudden feints and rallies, lyings down

in lying down and *maid, arise* arising
in fabulous yellows and greens and darker greens

and one might stand all day in love attending:
attending with precise and loving care

the motion of meaning in a field of grasses,
the sea beyond them and within them there

Who has taken from the dead men's eyes
the obols, sowing them in rows along
the tideline by the handful—small white
clamshells: *that thou givest me I gather:*
thou openest thine hand, I am filled with good;
thou hidest thy face, I am troubled: thou takest away....

The tide comes in, who hides the mudflats, up
and down the beach the pipers rise, resettle,
rise again: thou openest thine hand, they are filled
with good, they settle again in flocks to seek
their meat from thou to whom I don't know how
to make approach except by means of these

descriptions. A whimpering goes up from in their midst.
It's like an infant whimpering in her sleep.
It's fall, who's hung the apples, that thou givest
me I gather, in such kind ways you come
to me, I don't know how to come to you
except by means of these descriptions.

Who hast prepared a shelter for the fish
in the eagle's talons *(thou openest thine hand,*
I am filled with good); who huntst me in the last-
light through the spruce *(thou hidest thy face, I am troubled);*

who takest away...—in all such ways you come
to me. I don't know how to come to you

except by means of these descriptions, walking
to see you in the flesh along the wire
of my song, singing, *O thou who hearest
prayer, unto thee shall all flesh come.*

FOUNTAIN

Auden claimed
that he could hear,
in the murmuring
of underground streams,
a faultless love /
Or the life to come,
about either of which
he knew *nothing, Dear.*

Which comes of nothing.
Speak again:
the end-run round
the circle of
the garden closed,
the fountain sealed:
John Thompson's
learning by going;

how my speaking
threads the needle
of the pen,
the bone the ring,
nothing the circle
of my arms'
embrace of nothing:
nothing, flowing

BURNING THE LOVE LETTERS

Having on first reading
fed

the flames of early
love they're burning

now redundantly, but still give heat.
We fete

ourselves—still here, still
we—and feel

it, as those words turned flesh turn flame again—
and then

you turn to me: 'It's nice:
who burn their love letters warm themselves twice.'

ELEVEN TEXTS FOR UNACCOMPANIED VOICE

We hanged our harps upon the willows in the midst thereof.
(Psalm 137)

>   *I'm afraid*
> *at times,*
>   *of taking this harp*
> *down from the dead*
> *willow to sing*
> —Steven Heighton, 'A Psalm, on Second Thought'

    i.

At Princess Point in early fall
the willow leaves, bright yellow,
pave the ground by the shore of the lake
with gold, and we are here to take
some: stooping, gathering the swag
like oddsort cards into a bag.
Four months old, you hang on me
like a harp up in a willow tree,
in your egg-blue swaddle. I might sing:

    ii.

Knowing the way the world is bent,
knowing the hand, the harp's descent

from the bow (the way the mothers hunt
each other's young to feed their young),
knowing, always, that the hand
that rocks the cradle is the wind,
knowing the way the psalmist ends,
I am afraid to take these children
down from the dying willows, to sing.

iii.

Sing all a greene Willough must be my Garland.
Let no body blame him, his scorne I approue—
Nay that's not what follows next.
A willow grows aslant a brook
that *st*ews its tresses in the stream:
there with *gar*lands she did come,
clambering to hang them on
the boughs—one broke and down she tumbled.
With her garments spread around
her mermaidlike she drifted down
the river, writing poems like one
incapable of her own distress—
Nay, that's not what follows next.

iv.

It used to be nothing for me to swing
myself up by my skinny arms
into the crotch of an apple tree,
climbing where branches cradled me,

89

rocked by the wind that is the hand
that rules the world that rocks the wind.
Now I hesitate to lade
a tree that way. And know a cradle's
weight, and how the hand that rocks
the cradle rocks the cradle rocks
the cradle.

     v.

By the river the willows grow:
we hung our harps on the trees there so
we could sit and weep, remembering…. O,
they threw his head into the river
where it carries on, forever
singing; his harp into the sky.
Among the stars it's fallen silent,
though they say that it retains
its power to move the trees, the stones,
and even certain people— I'll
believe it when I see it. No, feel it.

     vi.

The lion, the lyre, the archer, the bow:
the hunter and the hunted. So.
She's up there still, the mama bear—
survives the god who assaulted her—
in a robe of stars and a coat of fur,
singing a song to her cub. It goes,

Under the willow Callisto stands
in her woman's weeds, her body of a bear sow:
Come on and tangle with me, Zeus,
Baby, if you dare, now.

    vii.

You're bigger now, although I keep
hoisting you up onto my hip
like a harp into a willow tree:
a harp that doesn't require me,
or anyone at all, to play.
She seized the harp and ran away,
but as she did, the instrument spoke,
saying, 'Master! Master!' and the giant woke....
A harp that doesn't require me,
or anyone at all, to play,
and when I set you down, you walk away.

    viii.

History does not record
what happened to those lyres stored—
no, shelved—upon the river willows.
Some claim to have heard them: still,
there is no reason to suppose
that they were taken down. Who knows?
To this day the willows weep:
as if in centuries of sleep
those cradled harps have grown into

the branches they were trusted to,
and weeping is the only song
they *can* sing, with the singers gone.

ix.

The leaves upon the ground are gold,
and also green, and yellow; and the older
ones have browned. And underneath,
still older ones have lost their teeth,
become a mesh of veins and stem,
or gone to the ground that gathers them.
Some verses back I said they are
a pavement. No: it is a carpet,
laid out on a ground with which
it comes to be continuous:
a substrate into which it turns.
A fire dying as it burns.

x.

When the giant came home he saw
the children playing in his garden.
'What are you doing here?' he cried,
and the children ran away, afraid,
and spring, too, fled the giant's yard.
One day he saw a boy too small
to reach the lowest branch for all
the tree bent down and bid him climb.
The giant rose and went to him,

and lifted the boy into the tree,
which broke into blossom instantly,
the blossoms overflowing now,
and falling to the ground—like snow.

xi.

Gathering leaves is work for Donne
or God, but without either one
I sort unnumbered pages, despair
of binding a fraction of what's here,
and leave the better part of them
upon the ground. And take you down.
And take you home.

I am true,
so I am fair:
the two are one.
I've got you there.

If I was fairly
false to you,
but beautifully:
were that not true?

Or let you see
my unkempt hair
au naturel:
were that not fair?

You're lucky I
see fit to cleave
to you, my love,
believe you me.

When I see you I think about my boys,
hungry. 'Nothing to have at heart.
It is to have or nothing,'
said Wallace Stevens,
in 'Poetry Is a Destructive Force.'

When I was pregnant I had my boys to heart.
Or nothing. I fed them, or nothing, from my body,
without trying. Without
this gloveless *keyless*
fumbling with my wallet *in the cold*

When what I wanted most—needed / most—
was to sieve you in.... In 'War on the Periphery,'
George Johnston wrote, 'My little
children eat
my heart.... They eat my heart and grow to men.'

Violent lovers, husbands, sons, when I
see you I think about my boys.

MERCY

Something there is that doesn't love a line
of verse, that sends the frozen ground-swell under
it, and spills the upper syllables in the sun.
I want to say it's poetry and yet it isn't poetry
exactly, this loving rearranger of the stones
so carefully laid—or not just poetry.
Time too misremembers: my
child's face revised from moment to moment.
And my own.
When I come to the river of memory, I want
to know the proper words; I don't.
Sometimes I have a perfect misrememory
of Carew: *When thou art troubled he shall hear and come
to thee, whose love embraced and didn't know his name.*

SONG

Never a summer's day: the fall,
the sweet birds giving
on bare choirs, choirs
choiring farewell,

and all things fair
from fair declining,
and declining
everywhere

thine absolute,
and absolute
for death. O thou,

to whom what is
is going, turn.
Approach me. Vernal. Here. Now.

IF YOU SEE ME FALL
after Se la face ay pale *(du Fay)*

If you see me fall
then you must believe
that the cause is love
and that love is all
that could make me fail,
founder in this sea—
and if I should leave
then the cause is love,
its billows and waves
gone over me.

If I seem to bear
more than mortal weight,
if I seem to wait
longer than is fair,
if I lie awake
know it is for him—
my beloved's voice
knocking at the door
calling me by name—
who is not there.

If I see your love
how am I to know?
Who is he that you
should be smitten so?
Has he eyes of doves,
are they fitly set,
that you washed his feet
with your woman's-hair?
He's the one you stare
past in the street.

RITUAL FOR MIDWINTER

Yes, let's begin anew:
lift the ashes in the grate,
there are living coals beneath.
The sun's light, banked, may reignite
and build again to summer's blaze.
Remember that? That's sunlight, banked.
Lift the ashes in the grate,
the old sun lifted clear of snow.

Born of Erebus and Night
and given neither wisdom nor
courage nor fore- or aftersight
but flawless aim and a mortal touch:
of Eros we know just this much,
which is enough. 'Twill serve, I'm peppered.
Bone rebound of bolt to bow:
of Eros this is all we know.

I didn't think it was an arrow
thrust him in. Some ointment, rather.
Spilled oil from a hidden lamp:
that's sunlight, banked. *A dog, a rat,*
a mouse, a cat, that fights by the book....
Seeing it was too late, she poured
out all the rest of the hoarded nard.
Which wasn't hers. But that didn't matter.

Severn, lift the ashes in

the grate. Let us begin again,
alone or married, children or not,
and who cares what profession. Say,
there is fresh snow to shovel, lift,
consign: *It is a snowy day.*
Lift the ashes in the grate.
There's a living sun beneath.

SHOWING

Having once been intimate
with everything, she found herself
unable to conceal it, sky-
blue vestments notwithstanding,
much less let it die: it grew in her;

and growing, insisted on being
born; and being born, on milk; and fed,
on speaking; and speaking, felled,
on what was clear from the beginning:
nowhere doesn't see this child.

FROST

if not a poem then perhaps
some darkened glass to interpose
between the one whose mortal cold
illuminates your breath and you
whose breath illuminates the cold—

I got me flowers to strew thy way;
I got me boughs off many a tree—

but thou wast up by break of day
illuminating all this speech,
the sun arising in the east,
and fire flowers opened there
and bloomed and died and the glass was clear

Trust who compose in darkness:
the return of light
is not to be
believed,

nor sought with lanterns. Lucie,
who scarce seaven
houres herself
unmaskes,

has darker sisters: who shows
her face scarce
six, scarce
five—

or not at all. When
the lamp's consumed
the oil, when
the lamp's

consumed even your hoarded
oil, you'll keep
her long night's
festivall.

Nor will my Sunne renew,
says Donne. Sit down,
wait: with him.
For the sun.

ET TANT M'EST AMER
after Baudelaire

1390   J. Gower *Confessio Amantis* ii. 186   In the virgine,
where he [the godhede] nome Oure flesshe and verray man
become Of bodely fraternite. *(Oxford English Dictionary)*

It's bittersweet on winter nights, from here—
sentenced to tend the palpitating hearth—
to hear out in the winterfog the bells
that call to mind for me the human heart.

Remember one who, notwithstanding age,
full-filled his spirit's emptiness with sound,
the new song that he promised long ago
sustained, refined, embellishèd, and loud?

Now he is flawed, and some velleity
hobbles his song before it outs from him
so that in his own ears it sounds of blood,
a stranded conch that will not chant its hymn.

Still, put this to your ear: *fraternite.*
The land of spices; something understood.

TREE

Circumdederunt me gemitus mortis, dolores
inferni circumdederunt me.

it's meet a Word
should hang upon
a tree, you wrote
I'll write it out

for you and hang it
on this tree
the one at the centre
of my story

     *

a story is
a circle its
circumference every-
where its centre

nowhere, no-
thing, nobody
says there is nothing
there's a tree

     *

look at the tree
a man-sized spruce
and decorated
by my son

with necklaces
a rosary
a tree on which
a tree is hung

                *

on which is hung
another tree
the circlet starred
with tiny beads

suspending its
small crucifix
I've laid it out
upon my desk

                *

we lay down there
upon my bed
all afternoon
in which He stood

attending with
precise and loving
care His very
flesh and blood

*

and at the centre
of each tree
there was a glade
that opened up

all of its own
accord as we
were speaking, Lover
look at me

O MAD BON MOT

There is no beauty, we are told,
that we should desire him—*non est species,*
neque decor—neither form
nor comeliness, and when he comes
at last he shall be poor
                 & for

the way the light comes walking toward
me on the water as I pray, as for the taper
of the dark hairs on your belly
toward your groin, it is a poor
Word, beauty, walking toward me

ITE, MISSA EST
for Christopher Snook, alive at sea

    i.

I went tonight and watched you celebrate
the Mass at King's, 'Perhaps for the last time,'
you said, '—or the first, with some new purpose,'
the Lord having survived in you the rainbow
of his will—and after that walked home.
The moon was high up in the sky above
the academic buildings and the streets
were quiet; a cold, still night.
                         Out
beyond the harbour bell the sea still breaks,
however, breaks—as on that night when the drowned
sailor clutched Lowell's drag-net. Nobody,
you said, can know the holiness of Advent
unless they've been beyond those farthest shelves,
that *brackish reach of shoal off Madaket,*
hauling in the net they've cast in horror,
hauling out the horror of themselves—

If God himself had not been on our side,
If God himself had not been on our side,
When the Atlantic rose against us, why,
Then it had swallowed us up quick.

It swallowed us up quick. Christopher,
when the Atlantic rose against us
did we grapple at the net—
or did we let ourselves be swallowed, let
ourselves be loved like that?

ii.

'Love's the boy stood on the burning deck,'
I tell my students: 'that's the first
of the half-dozen metaphors for love that Bishop
uses in this poem.' I write that first one
on the board. 'Now, what's the second?'

'The second one is *Love's the son...*':

                      'Yes!
What's the difference between these two?
Why has the boy become a son, by Bishop's
loving jugglery?'

            Her 'jugglery':
the word is Lowell's, from a letter he wrote
to that poor bastard faced with translating
his *Quaker Graveyard*—juggling its jugglery—
from English into Japanese. But Lowell
said his jugglery was bitter: *Hide*
our steel, Jonas Messias, in thy side.

iii.

'"Christ by my bitter jugglery becomes
the whale, not the Whaleman."' It's four thirty,
already the sky is dark outside, the night
has steamed into our North Atlantic city.
I am talking with a student whose copy
is barnacled with deftly pencilled characters,
devoutly marked: Korean? 'Everything
is everything,' I tell her. 'Christ
is, *pace* Lowell, both the whale *and* the whaleman—
the ship, . . . the swimming sailors who
would like a schoolroom platform, too—
the sea, all these. And God as well,
cause Love's the burning boy.' I tell her,
'That's the bitter jugglery of in-
carnation—which Mary knows. She knows
it in her bones, as one might know the text
of a well-loved poem, the sort that won't
desert one in extremis . . .':

If God himself had not been on our / hide
our steel Jonas Messias in your / Lady
hide us in your side . . . .

iv.

In my apartment on the hill
I wake to gulls and in their cries
I hear no trembling for the fact

of death in these home waters. No.
They scream for life. That urchin wrenched
from intertidal privacies and gut-
smashed on the rock: they don't
avert their gimlet eyes from that.
No, Sir. They lift it up.

v.

The world shall come to Walsingham.
I leave my office, five p.m., and night's
already steamed into our North Atlantic streets,
for it's December, sidewalk's icy, streetlights on...
and Giacometti's tree's become—
here in the building I call home—
the foyer's artificial fir.
How hard a path another's stair.

vi.

How salt the taste of others' bread.
Beyond my door I doff my shoes
and barefoot go the final mile
as pilgrims do, unto my bed.

At Easter you'll return to King's
in layman's clothes, without your wings.
You fear I will not know you then—
for after all you're just a man.

I think I'll recognize you there.
Will you know me without my hair?
Without my voice? Without my name?

Our ragged hearts are just the same.
I live in you and you in me,
and that's the loving jugglery.

NOTES AND ACKNOWLEDGEMENTS

Poems in this collection have been previously published in *Able Muse; Arc Poetry Magazine; The Fiddlehead; Cadence: voix féminines, Female Voices;* and *The Walrus.*

The Temple and *New Year Letter* were both given their first physical forms by Karen Schindler, who published them as chapbooks under her imprint Baseline Press, in 2018 and 2020/1 respectively.

'Fire Flower' was commissioned by the Art Gallery of Hamilton. It was originally published in *Rosemary Kilbourn: A Singular Place.*

Eleven Texts for Unaccompanied Voice was written for a paper made, bespoke, with willow-leaf inclusions, by Papeterie Saint-Armand.

The epigraph to 'The Documents' is copyright © 2015 by the Estate of W.H. Auden. Used with permission.

The epigraph to '*Et tant m'est amer*' is copyright © 2021 by the Oxford English Dictionary. Used with permission.

The second epigraph to *Eleven Texts for Unaccompanied Voice* is copyright © 2021 by Steven Heighton. Used with permission.

Many of these poems were written for music:

'Even So I'll Gather Roses,' *'Deus est sphaera cujus...,'* 'If You See Me Fall,' *Leçons de ténèbres, The Temple,* and *A Poor Passion* were all inspired and/or commissioned by Daniel Cabena.

'If You See Me Fall' was premiered by Daniel Cabena, Stephen Tok, and John Wiens as part of the Music at Noon series of the Faculty of Music, Wilfrid Laurier University, on land that is the traditional territory of the Neutral, Haudenosaunee, and Anishinaabe Peoples.

'Deus est sphaera cujus...' was workshopped with Daniel Cabena and members of the Beckett School Community Consort, on land that is the traditional territory of the Neutral, Haudenosaunee, and Anishinaabe Peoples; and in Mi'kma'ki, the ancestral and unceded territory of the Mi'kmaq People, in the fall of 2021.

The Temple was commissioned by Daniel Cabena and set to music by Zachary Wadsworth. The score (for SATB chorus; soprano, alto, and baritone soloists; string orchestra; oboe; and organ) is available online at zacharywadsworth.com/temple. The work was premiered by Spiritus Ensemble as part of the Ensemble's vespers service for the Feast of the Presentation on 28 January 2018, at St. John the Evangelist Church in Kitchener, Ontario, in the traditional territory of the Neutral, Haudenosaunee, and Anishinaabe Peoples.

A Poor Passion was developed with Daniel Cabena as part of
and emerging from our exploration of Oscar Wilde's prison
reading. This work was supported by the Canada Council for
the Arts.

We workshopped our *Passion* in Guelph, Ontario, in the
summer of 2020, on the traditional territory of the
Mississaugas of the Credit, with the support of Inter Arts
Matrix and of Mary Peirson. The performers were Daniel
Cabena, Sheila Dietrich, Chris Fischer, Daniel Lichti, Henry
Peirson, James McLennan, Terry McKenna, and Anna Ronai.
Workshop dramaturge was GaRRy Williams, and our musical
consultants were Tim Pyper and Zachary Wadsworth.

This book is full of the voices of interlocutors living and dead;
I acknowledge them here, as also those creatures who
nourished, those people who cared for my body, while the
words came to be in its midst.

I am grateful to the early readers of this book: Ali Blythe,
Daniel Cabena, Jon Claytor, Colleen (Coco) Collins, Jeffery
Donaldson, Jason Guriel, Melissa Hammell, Carey Jernigan,
shalan joudry, Gugu Hlongwane, Alexander MacLeod,
Emily Mernin, Suzanne Nussey, Ingrid Paulson, Raymond
Sewell, Carmine Starnino, John Sweet, Vanessa Stauffer,
Dan Wells...—thank you, miigwetch, wela'lin.

LUKE HATHAWAY is a trans poet who teaches English and Creative Writing at Saint Mary's University in Kjipuktuk/Halifax. He has been before now at some time boy and girl, bush, bird, and a mute fish in the sea. His book *Years, Months, and Days* was named a best book of 2018 in the *New York Times*. He mentors new librettists as a faculty member in the Amadeus Choir's Choral Composition Lab, and makes music with Daniel Cabena as part of the metamorphosing ensemble ANIMA.

MIX
Paper
FSC® C100212

Printed by Imprimerie Gauvin
Gatineau, Québec